Ancient Greek Women

Haydn Middleton

Heinemann Library
Chicago, Illinois

Designed by Tinstar Design
Illustration by Art Construction
Originated by Ambassador Litho
Printed by Wing King Tong in Hong Kong

07 06 05 04 03
10 9 8 7 6 5 4 3 2 1

Library of Congress Cataloging-in-Publication Data
Middleton, Haydn.
  Ancient Greek Women / Haydn Middleton.
      p. cm. -- (People in the past)
Includes bibliographical references and index.
  ISBN 1-58810-637-3 (HC) 1-4034-0135-7 (Pbk)
  1. Women--Greece--History--Juvenile literature. 2.
Women--Greece--Social conditions--Juvenile literature. 3.
Women--History--To 500--Juvenile literature. 4.
Greece--Civilization--Juvenile literature. [1. Women--Greece--Social
conditions. 2. Greece--Civilization.] I. Title. II. Series.
  HQ1134 .M53 2002
  305.42'0938--dc21
                    2001005216

Acknowledgments
The Publishers would like to thank the following for permission to reproduce photographs:
AKG London, pp. 6, 7, 12, 17, 18, 19, 24, 25, 26, 28, 39; Werner Forman Archive, pp. 8, 30; Ancient Art and Architecture Collection, pp. 10, 11, 15, 20, 22, 29, 32, 34, 36, 40, 42; Bildarchiv Performing Arts Library, p. 38; Preussischer Kulturbesitz, p. 43.

Cover photograph reproduced with permission of the Metropolitan Museum of Art.

Every effort has been made to contact copyright holders of any material reproduced in this book. Any omissions will be rectified in subsequent printings if notice is given to the publisher.

Some words are shown in bold, **like this.** You can find out what they mean by looking in the glossary.

Contents

"So Plato gave thanks to nature, first that he was born a human being rather than a dumb animal; second that he was born a man rather than a woman."

This was written by Lactantius, about the great **philosopher** Plato. Plato was by no means the only ancient Greek who believed that men were superior to women. Aristotle, who was famous for his scientific ideas, wrote, "A woman is … an imperfect male. She is female because her body is not properly made."

Plenty of other books and laws show a similar male attitude toward women. Unfortunately, hardly any writings by women about men have survived. In fact, we have hardly any writings by ancient Greek women about anything. As a result, we have very little evidence to tell us how ancient Greek women felt about their lives.

From Minoans to Macedonians

When people talk about ancient Greece, they do not mean just the modern country of Greece as we know it today. The ancient Greek world was made up of the hot, rocky mainland of Greece and hundreds of islands in the Aegean, Ionian, and Adriatic Seas, as well as further **colonies** overseas, in places ranging from northern Africa to what we now call Turkey and Italy. The earliest Greek speakers did not think that they all belonged to a single country. For a long time, they did not even think that they all belonged to the same **civilization.**

For centuries, the mightiest people in the Greek world were the Minoans, based on the island of Crete. Power then passed to the warlike Mycenaeans, based on the mainland in the region known as the **Peloponnese.** This was followed, around 1100 B.C.E., by three centuries of confusion and upheaval; since the art of writing was also lost, we know very little about it. Later, in the Classical Age, from about 500 B.C.E. to about 300 B.C.E., prosperity was restored by the rise to power of many long-lasting city-states, including Athens, Sparta, and Thebes. Most of the information in this book is about the life of women in such city-states during this period of Greek history.

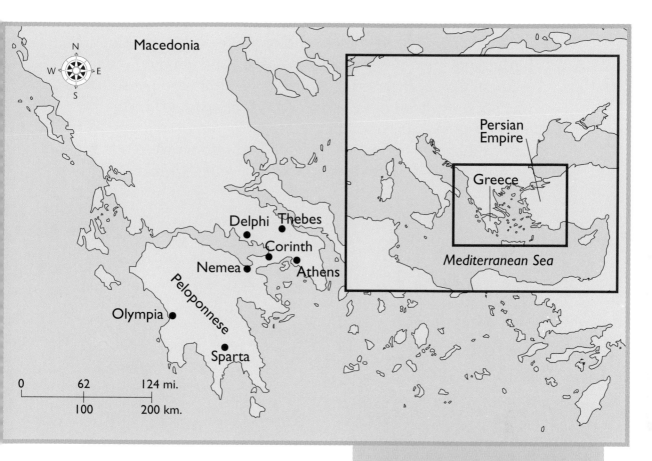

The Greek word for city-state is **polis.**
Each *polis* was a large city that
controlled the villages and farmland
around it. Each also had its own laws
and customs, and often they fought
bitter wars against each other. However,
all Greeks were united by their common
language and their belief that their ways

Ancient Greece was not a single,
unified country but was instead
a collection of many separate
states that varied greatly in size
and strength. The ancient Greeks
used the word *Hellas* to mean all
the places where there was a
Greek way of life.

were superior to those of any foreign **barbarians.** The quality of
many aspects of their civilization makes it hard to disagree. Ancient
Greek words, ideas, art forms, and attitudes still have a deep effect
on us all more than 2,000 years later.

A World of Opposites

Many ancient Greeks believed that the world was made up of opposites. There were Greeks and non-Greeks (whom they called **barbarians**), free people and slaves, right and left, and men and women. Greeks believed that, within each of these pairs, the first was not only different from the second but was also better. It is hard for us to understand this today. Nowadays, we know that men and women are equals. Yet the idea that women were not as good as men had a deep influence on life in ancient Greece.

Well-kept secrets

In reporting a speech by Pericles, the historian Thucydides recorded this statement about the place of women in ancient Greece: "If I am also to speak about feminine virtue … I can say all I have to say in one short word of advice. Your great glory is not to be inferior to the way nature made you; and the greatest glory is hers who is least talked about by men, whether in praise or in blame." Athenian men were expected to keep the names of their female family members secret from any men who were not related to them.

In Greek art, women were often shown to be smaller and less active than men. Usually women were shown indoors.

Some Greek men feared that there was a wild streak in all women. Images such as this suggested that women would act wild unless they were kept under strict control by men.

Different roles for men and women

As you will discover in this book, Greek writers and artists had strong views on the different roles that men and women had to play. While a man was expected to enjoy an active public life, a woman's place was thought to be in the home. Sometimes it may seem to you that women had a really hard time. Even in city-states such as Sparta, where women had more freedom, they were able to do and say far less than men.

Surviving sources tell us very little about everyday life in ancient Greece, and many of these sources tell us only how men wanted women to behave, not how women actually led their lives. We must use the evidence carefully if we are to glimpse what life was really like for women. We must also bear in mind that Greek men did not dislike or fear women—they just thought women were different. As Xenophon wrote: "The god of nature has given different kinds of beauty to us. It is his wish that the magnificence of the male should be admired by the female, and that the tender and curious touch of the female should be admired by the male."

Greek Girls

The two girls in the statue below are playing knucklebones, which was a popular game among Greek children. Girls also played with clay spinning tops, dolls, and rattles. We know this because such items are sometimes found by **archaeologists** in the graves of children who died young. Maybe they were placed there to be played with in the next world.

Just as they do today, the number of toys a girl had and the amount of time that she was allowed to play with toys depended on how wealthy her family was. The daughters of poor farmers had to work from a very early age, scaring birds away from crops or helping with the harvest. As they do today too, children kept pets—but ancient Greek children kept wild rabbits and quails instead of dogs and cats.

These girls are playing knucklebones. There were no mass-produced toys in ancient Greece, so children often had to make the best of what they could find.

Becoming an adult early

Childhood did not last long for boys or for girls. Boys went to school, but girls did not. Girls seem to have been brought up almost entirely inside their homes. There they learned the skills that they would one day need to run a household of their own. These skills included weaving, spinning, cooking, and caring for children.

From the age of about 13, girls were considered not to be children any more. During a special **ritual,** they dedicated all their toys to the goddess Artemis before putting them away forever. Girls married young and then continued the cycle by having babies themselves.

In some states, if a child was born weak or sickly, then its father could refuse to bring it up. A child that was refused by its father would then be left in a public place to die or, if the child was fortunate, to be found and adopted by someone else. It is possible that more baby girls than baby boys were treated in this way. Fathers may have welcomed boys, since they could go out into the world and bring fame or wealth back to the family. Most girls did not work for pay, so they had to be supported. From about 500 B.C.E., their families also had to provide them with a **dowry** before they could be married.

Girls on the left

Today, gynecology is the scientific study of women's bodies and diseases. It comes from the Greek word "gyne," meaning woman. Ancient Greek scientists had some strange ideas about what went on inside women's bodies. Baby girls were said to grow on the left side of the womb, while baby boys grew on the right. This supported the ancient Greek idea that boys and girls were opposites, like left and right.

Marriage

The author Xenophon wrote out a conversation between Ischomachos, a wealthy landowner, and the **philosopher** Socrates. "Pray tell me," asks Socrates, "did you instruct your wife how to manage your house, or was it her father and mother that gave her sufficient instructions to order a house before she came to you?" "My wife," answers Ischomachus, "was but 15 years old when I married her; and until then she had been so poorly brought up, that she hardly knew anything of worldly affairs." Isomachus was disappointed that he had to teach his wife how to manage his home. Greek wives were expected to run the household.

This is a picture of a wedding procession, by the Athenian painter Exekias, from about 540 B.C.E. Only rich newlyweds could afford horse-drawn chariots such as this. The rest had to be tugged along by less expensive mules or oxen.

Love *and* marriage?

In ancient Greece, fifteen years of age was not especially young for a bride. Grooms tended to be older, in their late twenties. Often, grooms were already close to the bride's family—perhaps a cousin or the father's best friend. Most marriages were arranged by parents, and a girl might be **betrothed** while still a child.

The ancient Greeks believed the purpose of being female was to be married, and the purpose of marriage was to have children to keep the family going. That might not sound very romantic. Indeed, few people seem to have married for love. One reason why a man married a girl was because she was expected to bring him a **dowry.** The richer the girl's family, the greater her dowry was likely to be. It could be as much as 10 percent of her father's wealth or property. Love sometimes came about after a marriage.

Inscriptions on tombs suggest that there could be affection between **spouses,** and in pictures of wedding ceremonies, the gods of love are often shown. These ceremonies did not take place in temples. The groom fetched the bride from her home and took her back to his family's house in a chariot or cart . There the groom's parents met them, led them to the **hearth**—the symbol of family life—and showered them with fruit and nuts. The couple knelt by the fire to say prayers. The next day there was a feast with gift giving.

Early ends to marriage

Since a bride was usually much younger than her new husband, she was often the youngest person in her new household. It must have been hard to adjust, especially since she had to spend so much time indoors. For marriages that did not work, divorce was a way out. If a man divorced his wife, then he had to pay back her dowry, and she normally returned to her own family home. If the father of an **heiress** died, however, Athenian law said that she had to divorce her husband and then marry her nearest available relative, to make sure that all her father's property would not be given away to distant family members.

This *loutrophoros* pot was used to fill the **ritual** bath of a bride before her wedding. A pot like this might also be placed on the grave of a woman who never got married, as a marker.

Life as a Wife

"There is one prime source of scandal
for a woman: when she won't stay indoors.
I longed to go out, but no! I stayed at home
and indoors I did not practice saucy speech,
like some women. My mind, sound by nature,
was my teacher. I needed no more.
I offered my husband a silent tongue
and gentle looks. I knew when to have my way and
when to let him have his."

This speech tells us a lot about women's roles in Greek families. It is made by the character Andromache in *The Women of Troy*, a play written by Euripedes. The playwright, a man, was putting words into the mouth of a woman. Women were expected to stay indoors and to stay quiet while they managed their husbands' households. Andromache, however, suggests that she knew how to manage her husband too—by letting him have his way, and knowing when to have her own.

Here a Greek woman washes and beautifies herself. In her domestic setting, a Greek wife and mother was respected, but she was given little chance to be seen or heard outdoors.

Some women may have had quite a lot of power at home. We cannot say for sure, since there is so little surviving evidence. In Xenophon's play *Oeconomicus*, Socrates asks Kritoboulos, "Is there anyone to whom you commit more affairs of importance than to your wife." "No," he replies. Then Socrates asks, "Is there anyone to whom you talk less?" "Few or none," he admits. This suggests that Kritoboulos was quite happy to leave the organization of his home to his wife.

Busy as bees

The poet Semonides of Amorgos likened women to different animals. According to him, only a woman like a bee is any good for a man: "She causes his property to grow and increase, and she grows old with a husband whom she loves and who loves her, the mother of a handsome and **reputable** family. She stands out among all women, and a godlike beauty plays around her. She takes no pleasure in sitting among women in places where they tell stories about love." Bees, of course, are famously busy—and wives and mothers, whether rich or poor, worked hard to run a household. There would have been little time for them to do jobs outside the home or to get involved in politics. This suited many men perfectly. For they believed that the temptations of the outside world would be too strong for most women to resist.

Mothers

"Plainly," wrote Xenophon in *Memorabilia*, "we look to wives who will produce the best children for us, and marry them to raise a family…. She cares for the baby night and day laboriously for a long period, and with no expectation of reward." A Greek woman might have six or seven pregnancies, but as many as one in three babies died in their first year. Poor women, unable to afford the expense of caring for them, sometimes gave up their babies for adoption.

Running the Home

The Greek word for a home was *oikos*. The materials used to build the home were also called *oikos,* and the same word was used for the family. Today, we might use the word "household" to mean something similar. Under a single roof there might sometimes be three generations: grandparents, a married son and his wife, and their children. In larger homes, there might be even more relatives, including those who were either unmarried, widowed, or divorced. Although the head of the *oikos* was always a man, the task of making it run smoothly fell to the women—whether they were members of the family or, in richer homes, servants or slaves.

Andron and *gunaikon*

On the following pages, you can find out what jobs women had to do or supervise. They did their work in several different kinds of homes, but in many, the women's own quarters were **segregated** from the men's more public areas—especially the *andron*, where male guests were entertained.

The women's area of the house was called the *gunaikon*. In bigger Athenian houses, women's rooms were not near the street entrance, which might be guarded by a slave. In country farmhouses, there were courtyards where the women and children lived by day, surrounded by single-story rooms. In one corner, there might be a storage tower. If a stranger or male visitor came, the women would go upstairs and wait in the tower.

Women below

"I have a small two-story house, with the women's quarters upstairs, the men's downstairs, each having equal space. When our son was born, his mother nursed him; but in order that she might avoid the risk of climbing downstairs each time she had to feed the baby, I used to live upstairs and the women below. It became customary for my wife to go downstairs often and sleep with the child, so that she could ... keep him from crying," one ancient Greek father wrote.

This seated woman must have been quite wealthy, since she is being waited on by a female servant. Rich wives were expected to train and supervise their domestic staff. "We're always dancing attendance on our husbands," says a character in Aristophanes' play *Lysistrata*, "or getting the maid moving, or putting the baby to bed, bathing it, feeding it."

Cooking

The women's quarters in a Greek house included the cooking area. Men, servants, or slaves went shopping for food, but women did most of the cooking. In towns, women had to make bread, which was a vital part of the ancient Greeks' diet, from barley. "Take care that the corn which is brought in," Ischomachus advised his wife in Xenophon's *Oeconomicus*, "is not laid up in such a manner that it grows musty and unfit for use." Barley was usually soaked and toasted before it was turned into porridge or cakes. A bride might bring a barley-roasting pan to her wedding.

Women from reasonably wealthy families prepared only one big meal a day. This meal was called the *deipnon* and was eaten in the late afternoon. The first course might consist of poultry or fish, perhaps with some cheese, and was accompanied by sauces and vegetables such as lentils, celery, radishes, and beans. A second course could include figs, olives, grapes, nuts, and other fruit. Cattle were in short supply, and meat of any kind was usually eaten only at the feasts that were held after **sacrifices.**

How to eat and drink

Greek people followed various **rituals** for eating and drinking. The **philosopher** Plutarch said that, when he was growing up, girls and boys were trained to take bread with the left hand and *opson* (almost everything else) with the right. There was also no shortage of advice on how to drink the strong, gritty wine.

Women drank water, wine, or, more often, a mixture of the two. Sometimes they drank in the company of men, but they were seldom invited to parties called *symposia*, which could get a little wild. Women were supposed to drink enough diluted wine to make them feel relaxed and chatty but not so much that it made them "stupid."

Finding the right balance

Women had to take care about what types of food they put together and exactly how they cooked them. The ancient Greeks believed that each dish had a particular "power" over the body: moistening, drying, or heating. Unfortunately, not everyone agreed about which foods had which powers!

Women who could afford it used honey in their cooking. The god Zeus was said to have been brought up on honey and goat's milk.

Women from all backgrounds were likely to include fish in their menus. From anchovies to tuna, sea bass, and eels, so many fish were caught around Greece that they were relatively cheap.

This statue shows a Greek woman preparing a meal. There were few labor-saving devices in the kitchens of the ancient world, although slaves and servants did some of the more demanding work.

Weaving and Sewing

In ancient Greek mythology, there were three sister goddesses who were known as the Fates. These three Fates were in charge of human destiny. Clotho spun out the thread of each person's life, Lachesis measured how long that thread should be, and Atropos chose when to cut it and so bring death.

Wool and women

For **mortal** Greek women, spinning and weaving were very important occupations in the home. Although the rich might buy clothes of linen, hemp, flax, or silk, many ordinary Greek families kept a few sheep to provide wool from which to make their own clothing. The women of the household would dye the wool and would spin it into **yarn** before weaving it into cloth to make whatever was needed. In addition to clothing, women made wall hangings, floor coverings, and bedding.

Not all cloth was made in the home by women. Some was made in small "factories" in which men worked too—however, wool was usually thought of as something women worked with.

In Athens, when a baby girl was born, a **fillet** of cloth was attached to the house's main door to announce the news. Athenian women also took part in the *Panathenaea* festival each year by weaving a new dress for Athena, the city's goddess and protector.

Images such as this one on a vase often showed women in the home, spinning or weaving.

Penelope's deception

Women wove cloth by standing or sitting at upright wooden **looms.** It could take a long time. In one Greek myth, Odysseus, the King of Ithaca, was away from his wife Penelope for twenty years. Many suitors gathered at her palace, saying he must be dead and hoping to marry her in his place. Penelope said she would choose a new husband when she had finished weaving a **shroud** for Odysseus's father. Each day she worked at her loom, but each night in secret she unpicked her day's work. By doing this, she played for time, and in the end Odysseus returned to her.

This decorated item was called an *epinetron*. Women used it to tease out tangled wool before they started to spin it.

Work Outside the Home

The wives of wealthy Greek men rarely left their homes. Their husbands thought it far too risky. According to the playwright Aristophanes, if a woman even stood at her doorway looking out on the street, then she was thought to be tempting men to come inside. Aristotle wrote that, in some Greek cities, officials called *gunaikonomoi* supervised wealthy women and made sure that they stayed indoors. Such women would not even visit the market to buy fresh food or barley to make bread. These jobs would instead be done by the men in their household, or by servants and slaves.

This young woman is entertaining a group of men by playing a wind instrument. Other ancient Greek paintings show female musicians playing handheld harps and dancers performing expressive steps.

Citizens and slaves

In 5th-century-B.C.E. Athens, there were between 80,000 and 100,000 slaves. That was one slave for every free member of the population. Most of them were foreigners, such as **Persians** captured during warfare. Others were the children of slaves.

Slaves in Sparta, Thessaly, or Sicily often led hard lives, but in Athens, it might be difficult to tell who was a slave and who was free. At the marketplace, slaves rubbed shoulders with poor women who had no one to run their errands for them. Sometimes, to make money, these poor women sold food from their family gardens at the market. They might also work outside the home as cooks, cleaners, nannies, **wet nurses**, or grape pickers.

Poor women might perform in other people's homes as paid dancers or musicians. Some women played an instrument called an *aulos*, which was something like a modern oboe. At the lower end of its range, the Greeks said it sounded like the buzzing of wasps, while on the high notes it was like the honking of geese. Men were still happy to pay to hear it played.

Disgracing the family

Slaves and women did not qualify as **citizens** and were not allowed to vote. This meant that they had no say in how their city-state was run. Citizens and their families were not supposed to work outside the home. However, in times of crisis and hardship, some citizens did have to work to provide for their families. If respectable women worked, it could damage the whole family's reputation. At the end of the **Peloponnesian** War with Sparta, it was discovered that the mother of an Athenian, Euxitheous, had been working as a wet nurse. As a result, Euxitheous was struck off the register of citizens. "You will find many Athenian citizens acting as wet-nurses today," Euxitheous protested.

Celebrations

▶◀▶ ◀▶ ◀▶ ◀▶ ◀▶ ◀▶ ◀▶ ◀▶ ◀▶ ◀▶ ◀▶ ◀▶ ◀▶ ◀▶ ◀▶ ◀▶ ◀

Life for Greek women did not always mean all work and no play. But since their husbands preferred them not to go out, what did they do for entertainment? Men were able to go to the theater—to watch plays written by men be performed by men. Women were not supposed to be in these audiences, yet Plato wrote that some "refined women" did watch public plays and that they preferred **tragedies** to comedies.

One of the few reasons that women were allowed to leave the house was for religious festivals. This carving shows a group of women dancing in a religious ceremony. The man playing the pipes is a representation of the god Dionysis, who was being celebrated in this particular festival.

Mystery festival

Most women probably enjoyed themselves by visiting or being visited by female friends and relatives. In the privacy of their own homes, they could be more at ease. How *much* they more at ease they could be is another matter. Male Greek writers thought that women lacked any self-control and said that they easily fell in love or got drunk. Can we believe this? Aristotle said that in Sparta, where women had more freedom, "women live without restraint, enjoying every **license** and indulging in every luxury."

Holy dances

The ancient Greeks believed that they had invented dancing. Women did not dance in a casual way, but at religious festivals, they performed in public and enjoyed watching others perform. Sometimes women danced in processions to the temples of the gods. The celebrations might also include singing, drinking wine, and eating barley cakes. Women were especially important in honoring the god Dionysus. They performing an outdoor dance that followed a winding torchlit path through the trees to the top of a mountain.

Men were also suspicious about what went on at all-female festivals such as the *Thesmophoria*. In a play by Aristophanes, a man dresses as a woman and tries to take part. The women will not let him, unless he can say what happens at the festival:

> *Women*: Tell me, what do we do first as part of the holy **rites**?
> *Man:* Um, let me see, what is it first?—we drink.
> *Women:* Well, what do we do after that?
> *Man*: We drink.
> *Women:* Someone must have been letting on to you....

Aristophanes was only guessing what happened at the festival. Even today we have no real idea what happened there. We do have a clearer picture of how men relaxed. At their all-male dinner parties, female musicians would sometimes perform for the guests, playing wind or stringed instruments. At least these women were given the chance to get out of the house.

What They Wore

Paintings and figures from ancient times clearly show what Greek women wore. Male artists often showed boys and men naked, but they almost always showed women with their clothes on. This may have meant that they believed women's bodies were shameful or unattractive, or it may have meant they found women even more attractive when they were kept from view.

The classical style

Ancient Greece was a hot place. Many Greek women just wore a *chiton*, which was a long, sleeveless, loose-fitting linen **shift** that sometimes had a pattern on it. It was held in place by brooches at the shoulder and a belt at or above the waist. This produced the folds often shown in Greek sculpture. In colder weather, wealthy women might add a square of woolen cloth on top, as a cloak. This was called a *himation*. On their feet, women wore simple leather sandals with nailed soles, which were made by a local cobbler. Wealthier women had their clothes made for them and had a number of different outfits from which to choose. Most women made their own clothes, and did not have many outfits.

We can get clues about what women wore from sculptures such as these, from the Erechtheion, a temple built high above Athens.

This vase painting shows women harvesting fruit. The robes that they are wearing are typical of the everyday dresses worn by women in ancient Greece.

Women's clothes were fairly loose and shapeless, unlike those of **barbarians,** who were often shown in tight-fitting outfits that showed off their bodies. Variety in dress came from using different materials and decorative styles. For example, a *chiton* might be made from hemp, linen, silk, or wool and might be striped, spotted, or bordered. Colors also varied—yellow was thought to be a woman's color.

As we do today, some people used tricks to improve their appearances. The following comes from *Fair Measures,* by the comic poet Alexis: "One is rather short. A cork sole is stitched into her shoes. One is too tall. She wears thin slippers…. One has no hips. She sews on a bustle under her dress." Xenophon advised against paying attention to any sort of clothing: "Those who study nothing but their dress may be esteemed by those who understand nothing else. But the outside appearance is deceitful."

Unsuitably dressed

According to one Greek source, if a woman was seen on the streets of Athens in "unsuitable" clothing, she could be made to pay a fine of 1,000 *drachmas*. We cannot be sure what clothing was suitable, but it was probably anything that kept the body well covered. The **philosopher** Socrates once argued with his wife Xanthippe because she refused to wear his big cloak when going out to watch a festival procession. When women took part in weddings or great festivals in public, they dressed up in fine clothes, gold, and jewels.

Beauty Tips

Helen, one of the most famous women in Greek myths, was described as "The face that launched a thousand ships, and burned the topless towers of Ilium." She was so beautiful that a quarrel over who should be her husband sparked off the ten-year-long war between Greece and Troy (or Ilium). So how did real ancient Greek women beautify themselves? As usual, men had their own ideas.

Keep it simple

Xenophon's Ischomachus liked the clean and simple look: "Men always prefer that body which is most pure, or the least deformed by art." He recommended housework to make a woman look

It is impossible to know whether the artist intended to show either how lovely this Greek woman looked or how vain she was about her appearance. Some male writers seemed to prefer women with a more natural look.

"more healthful … and add to the bloom" of her beauty. Then, "the clean appearance of the mistress among the servants … will encourage them to follow her example." Aristophanes wrote that some women wore so many ornaments that it was impossible to list them all: "Some face powder, some scent … a veil, some **rouge,** two necklaces, some eye paint … a hair-net … earrings, a pendant, more earrings … pins, necklace, bracelet, bangles … anklets, seals, chains, rings … more earrings—it's past man's power to tell you all the things."

Men had clear ideas on the skin tone of women too. The Greeks believed that women took in more moisture from their food, so their flesh was "wetter and wool-like." Also, as you can see in paintings, Greek men are usually shown with darker skins, while Greek women and "womanish" **barbarians** are shown with pale, white skin. Maybe men wanted to keep women indoors to keep them from getting suntans.

Women wore perfume from little bottles called *aryballoi*. The perfume was made from olive oil and herbs. Unless they were slaves, women wore their hair long—in ringlets before they were married, then piled up with ribbons and metal decorations afterward. Just like today, styles and lengths went in and out of fashion.

Keeping up appearances

In *Fair Measures*, the comic poet Alexis described, in the somewhat mean-spirited passage following, how some women tried to disguise flaws in how they looked, while others made the best of their looks:

"One has blonde eyebrows. She paints them with lampblack.

"One is too dark-complexioned; she is smeared with white-lead.

"One is too pale; she applies rouge.

"One is beautiful—in part. That part is revealed bare.

"One has attractive teeth. She must always be laughing so that those present can see what a nice mouth she has.

"If she doesn't want to laugh, she has to spend the whole day indoors, and … has to keep a slim stick of **myrtle** vertically between her lips, till as time passes, she's grinning whether she wants to or not."

Goddesses

"All things," said the **philosopher** Thales, "are full of gods." The people of ancient Greece worshiped many different **deities,** some of which were private or local and others of which ruled over the entire Greek world. The Greeks believed that six major gods and six major goddesses lived on Mount Olympus, the highest mountain in Greece at 9,570 feet (2,917 meters).

Both men and women prayed to the goddesses—Hera, Athena, Aphrodite, Demeter, Artemis, and Hestia—but all six goddesses had special powers for women. Hera, Zeus's wife and queen of the gods, was the guardian of faithful wives. Athena watched over crafts such as spinning and weaving, among other duties. Aphrodite was the goddess of love. Demeter, the goddess of fertility, made sure that the earth brought forth an abundance of crops. Artemis protected unmarried girls and watched over women in childbirth. Hestia, the goddess of the **hearth,** watched over the most important place in most women's lives, the home. From the many myths that feature these goddesses, we can gather what ideal Greek women were supposed to be like.

This statue, from about 130 B.C.E., shows the Venus de Milo. *Milo* was the Roman name for Melos, the Greek island where the statue was found, and *Venus* was the Roman name for Aphrodite, the Greek goddess of love.

The judgment of Paris

In a famous Greek myth, Paris, the handsome son of the King of Troy, is given a golden apple. He is told by the god Mercury to give it to the most beautiful of three goddesses: Athena, Hera, or Aphrodite. Each goddess, desperate to win, offers Paris a gift if he will pick her. Athena says she will make him invincible in battle. Hera promises to make him lord over all men. Aphrodite says she will give him the loveliest of all **mortal** women, Helen, to be his wife. Paris picks Aphrodite and gives her the apple. Soon afterward, he meets Helen, who is already married to the Greek King Menelaus, seizes her, and takes her back to Troy. The kidnapping of Helen resulted in the ten-year-long Trojan War. The Greeks sometimes used myths like this to explain real-life events.

Guardian of Greece's greatest city

Although the women of Athens had no say in the running of their city, its **patron** was a female deity, Athena. As the goddess of wisdom and warfare, she was supposed to ensure that the men of Athens governed wisely and fought well. The Greek sculptor Phidias made a famous statue of Athena, which was 39 feet (12 meters) high and covered in gold, ivory, and colored stones. This statue stood in the Parthenon.

Athena herself had no real mother. To be a true Athenian **citizen,** and be allowed to vote in elections and to help run the city, a man had to have both an Athenian father and an Athenian mother.

This vase shows the goddess Athena, who, according to legend, was born fully formed and dressed in armor, from the head of her father, Zeus.

Troublemakers

This painting shows Odysseus tied to the ship's mast by his own men. He was the first man to hear the song of the female Sirens and live to tell the tale.

This picture shows a scene from a Greek myth. The hero of this myth is Odysseus, King of Ithaca. His thrilling story is told in *The Odyssey,* by the poet Homer, who probably wrote between 800 and 700 B.C.E. Odysseus has several encounters with female troublemakers. In this scene, he has asked to be tied to the mast, for he knows that beautiful creatures called Sirens lure sailors to their doom with irresistible songs. Odysseus wants to hear the Sirens without being lured to go to them. The men in his crew have their ears stuffed with beeswax so that they cannot hear.

Fierce women

Myths explore people's deepest fears and longings. In the Greek myths, men often described what they thought women might be like if they were not kept under strict control. The beautiful, **seductive,** but evil Sirens are an example.

Another nightmare figure was Medusa—a female Gorgon with snakes for hair and a mouth filled with tusks. Anyone who looked her in the face was turned to stone. The Greeks also told stories about the Harpies, enormous birds with women's faces and long, hooked claws. They swooped down to ruin the food people were eating and sometimes carried off the people themselves. Other myths introduced the Amazons, women warriors who were considered manly because of their courage. There were no men in their nation. When an Amazon gave birth to a son, he was either killed or sent to live with his father, in a neighboring country.

Giving in to temptation

Pandora, believed by the Greeks to be the first **mortal** woman, was created by several **deities.** Zeus gave her either a jar or a box, which he ordered her never to open. Once on Earth, she married a man called Epimetheus, but she could not resist the temptation to look inside the box and see what was inside. As soon as she opened the box, Disease, War, Famine, and other evils poured out, to trouble the world forever after. Only blind Hope remained, to bring comfort to troubled humankind. One message of this Greek myth is that women are responsible for all of the bad things in the world.

Stories about women such as these were supposed to be entertaining. They also served as warnings about the dangers that lurk in all women. The moral of these stories was that men had to keep women in their place, or terrible things would happen.

Women in Public

▶◀▷ ◀▷ ◀▷ ◀▷ ◀▷ ◀▷ ◀▷ ◀▷ ◀▷ ◀▷ ◀▷ ◀▷ ◀▷ ◀▷ ◀▷ ◀▷ ◀▷ ◀

Greek women were believed to be weaker than men—more emotional, less **rational,** and therefore more prone to wild behavior. This generally led men to keep them closely supervised. However, on some occasions the "weaknesses" of women came in handy. At funerals and religious festivals, they could express their emotions in public, while the men would have to keep up their strong, "manly" appearances.

These women are tying ribbons to a tombstone as part of a funeral ceremony.

Honoring the gods

Many different local and national festivals were held in honor of the Greek **deities.** The Greeks believed that the gods and goddesses watched over these festivals and treated the people who took part more favorably. Women played a major role in many of the **rituals.** The great *Thesmophoria* festival, which was held in Athens over three days each fall, was celebrated only by women. At the *Arrephoria*, unmarried girls celebrated **rites** to encourage fertility. Around 150 B.C.E., the author Pausanias, in *A Guide to Greece*, described these rites:

"Two girls live near the temple of Polias; the Athenians call them *Arrephoroi*. They live with the goddess for a time. When the festival comes they perform the following ritual by night. They set on their heads objects given them to carry by the priestess of Athena; the nature of these objects is not known to either giver or bearers. Now there is within the city not far away an enclosure dedicated to the goddess called Aphrodite in the Gardens, and there is a natural underground passage leading down through it. The girls make their descent by this. They leave down below the objects they are carrying, and bring back something else which is carefully wrapped up. The girls are then dismissed." This rite, which was probably very scary, was definitely women's work in the eyes of many Greek men.

Funeral practices

Greek art clearly shows that women took the role as **mourners** during funeral processions to the cemetery. Laws were passed in Athens to limit women's **lamentations** for the dead, for fear that women mourners might cause a public disturbance. Euripides described women mourners in this way: "Mothers have lost their children, maidens have cut their hair in mourning for their brothers.... Hands are laid to the head; fingernails tear the delicate skin of the cheek which is wet from the flowing of blood." By contrast, the men stayed largely silent while the body was laid out to be visited by people paying their last respects and then taken to the cemetery for burial.

Women at the Olympics

A large athletic festival took place every four years to honor the god Zeus. Since it was held at Olympia, in the **Peloponnese,** it became known as the Olympic Games. According to tradition, the Olympic Games were founded by Heracles, and the first Olympic champion was Coroebus of Elis, a local cook who won the sprint race in 776 B.C.E. Coroebus was a man, and so were all the other competitors, including runners, jumpers, chariot racers, horse racers, boxers, wrestlers, discus throwers, and javelin throwers. The spectators were men, also.

Apart from a few priestesses, women were most definitely not welcome. Even women who were the owners of chariots or horses were forbidden to enter the sacred arena to watch their teams compete.

A girl athlete in Sparta would have been given more freedom to participate and compete in athletic events than girls elsewhere in Greece. The Spartans believed that, if girls trained hard, then they would make themselves strong for childbirth when they were older.

Crazy Callipateira

Since their presence was seen as **sacrilegious,** any woman who was caught in the crowd at the Olympic Games could be punished by execution. However, this did not frighten one woman, whose story was told by several Greek writers.

Callipateira of Rhodes belonged to a family of successful athletes in the 5th century B.C.E. Her father and her three brothers all won Olympic crowns. Eventually, her own son, Eukles, showed great promise as a boxer. Callipateira longed to see him compete in the Olympic Games, so she dressed herself as a male trainer and slipped into the stadium. When Eukles became the Olympic champion, Callipateira could not contain her joy. She leapt out of the crowd to embrace her beloved son—and revealed herself to be a woman.

The officials debated what to do with her. In the end, they let her go home, because of their respect for her distinguished family. However, from that point onward, all trainers had to be naked, to prevent any more deception. This was not as startling as it may sound today, since all the athletes were naked while they competed.

Female athletes

At the ancient Olympic Games, only men were allowed to compete for prizes and glory. There were races for young women at other times. At Olympia, there was a very old temple to the goddess Hera, the wife of Zeus. The temple's officials trained girl athletes, who ran short races in honor of the goddess. Women did finally make it into the Olympic Games—but they had to wait until the 20th century before men let them in. The ancient Olympics were abolished in 393 C.E. and were revived as an international competition in 1896. At the first modern Olympic Games, held in Athens in 1896, only men were allowed to participate. Women athletes competed in the Olympic Games for the first time in 1900.

Famous Women

In public, Greek men were not supposed to discuss the women in their household or family. Even saying the women's names was **taboo.** Perhaps because of this, male Greek writers have left us with very few descriptions of the lives of real women, but we do know about three women: Xanthippe, Aspasia, and Sappho.

Many stories were told about Xanthippe, the nagging wife of the **philosopher** Socrates. He often seemed ashamed of her. On the morning before Socrates was to be executed, wrote Plato, "we went in and found Xanthippe sitting by him with their child in her arms. When Xanthippe saw us she burst out with the sort of sentiments women will produce: 'Socrates, this is the last time you and your friends will talk together.' Socrates looked toward Crito and said, 'Crito, someone had better take her home.'"

This Athenian vase from the 5th century B.C.E. shows Sappho, the celebrated female poet from the island of Lesbos. Her skills were valued so highly that parents living elsewhere in Greece sent their daughters to be taught by her.

Aspasia and Sappho

Aspasia lived in Athens in the 5th century B.C.E. An intelligent, strong-minded woman, she entertained many great Athenian men in her home—and, unusually for that time, took part in their conversations. One of these men, the political leader Pericles, fell in love with her, divorced his wife, and set up a new home with Aspasia. People believed that she helped him to write many of his great speeches. To some men, this did not seem like a suitable role for a woman, and they criticized her bitterly. Yet Pericles stood by her until his death. "Every day," wrote Plutarch, "on leaving for his public business and on returning he would kiss her."

Sappho, a poet, was one of the rare Greek woman whose own writings have survived. We know only a little about her life: she was born in about 600 B.C.E. on the island of Lesbos, and she was married and had a daughter. Her poems were praised in her lifetime and have inspired many other great writers, both ancient and modern.

Passionate poetry

Here is one of Sappho's most famous love poems:

"Whenever I look at you even quickly

it is no longer possible to speak,

but my tongue fixes, and at once

a delicate fire flickers under my skin.

"I no longer see with my eyes, my ears hum,

sweat trickles down me, trembling seizes me all over,

I am paler than grass, and I seem to be

little short of dying."

Another fragment, found on **papyrus** and also about love, begins like this:

"Some say that the most beautiful thing on this dark earth

is a squadron of cavalry, others say

a troop of infantry, others a fleet of ships:

but I say that it is the one you love."

Tragic Women

▶◀▶ ◀▶ ◀▶ ◀▶ ◀▶ ◀▶ ◀▶ ◀▶ ◀▶ ◀▶ ◀▶ ◀▶ ◀▶ ◀▶ ◀▶ ◀▶

Kreousa, a female character in *Ion*, a play by Euripedes, says, "The lot of women is troublesome to men and since the good are confused with the bad, we are all hated. Thus we are born unlucky." Kreousa is a fictional character, but, as do characters in many Greek plays, she gives us a glimpse of how ancient Greek women saw their lives.

In *Tereus*, a **tragedy** by Sophocles, Procne makes this sad speech: "In my opinion young girls have the sweetest existence known to **mortals** in their fathers' homes—innocent, safe, and happy always. But when we grow a little older, we are sold away into marriage. Some go to strangers' homes, others to foreigners', some to joyless houses, some to hostile. As soon as we have been married to our husbands, we are forced to say all is well."

This photograph shows the actress Fiona Shaw as Medea, in a modern version of Euripides' play about a woman who murders her children.

The outsider

In his play about Medea, a character in ancient Greek myths, Euripides showed how wild a woman could be. Medea killed her own children to punish her husband, Jason, for abandoning her. Euripides put words into Medea's mouth that expressed how hard women's lives were. Medea was a foreigner, so she was called a **barbarian,** or an outsider among the Greeks. Many ancient Greek plays showed all women, not only foreigners, being treated like outsiders. They showed women as villains who threatened the civilized world of men.

Women's difficult lives

In this speech from the play by Euripides, Medea speaks out about the hardships that many Greek women suffered:

"Of all creatures that feel and think,
we women are the unhappiest species …
When the man tires of the company of his wife,
he goes outside and relieves the burden of his heart
and turns to a friend or companion of his own age.
But we are forced to keep our eyes on one alone.
They say that we women have a safe life at home,
while men must go to war. Nonsense!
I would rather fight in battle three times
than go through childbirth once."

The character Medea continues to haunt the imaginations of artists and authors in modern times. In 1998, the German author Christa Wolf wrote a novel about the Medea myth.

Did Women Get a Fair Deal?

The women of Athens had fewer rights than most women today. They were not supposed to leave the home, let alone get jobs or have a say in the way in which the **polis** was governed. Women were not allowed to vote, nor were they allowed to speak at the public **assembly.** They were not even allowed to enter the law courts. For their entire lives, they were forced to obey a male guardian. When a woman got married, her dependence was passed from their father, or her closest male relative, to her husband. If women got divorced or were widowed, then they had to go back under the control of the men in their family. The only advantage that women had over men was that they did not have to fight in wars.

This woman is shown in a pose that is respectful toward a man. From the time she was born, an ancient Greek woman would have to obey the male head of her household.

The Spartan exception

In most of ancient Greece, women had a similar **status.** A woman's guardian had to feed, clothe, and protect her, and in return she was treated as a piece of his property.

It was, however, a different story in the *polis* of Sparta. There, since men of up to 30 years of age lived together in special military **barracks,** many women had to manage their households alone. They could own land and property, they could take part openly in outdoor sports, and they could even express their views on current affairs. The Athenian thinker Aristotle was disgusted by the freedoms given to Spartan women: "At Sparta women live without restraint, enjoying every **license** and indulging in every luxury. One inevitable result is that great importance is attached to being rich, particularly in communities where the men are dominated by the women."

To us, it seems that most ancient Greek women were treated as second-class citizens. Many women today would find it hard to live under such conditions. However, it is important to remember that ancient Greek women did not know any other way of life. We can try to guess what Greek women thought about their lives, but since so little hard evidence of their views survives, we cannot know for certain.

The value of discipline

Greek men believed in discipline. Men and women both needed discipline, for without it, they feared, there would be chaos in the world. Yet while men believed that they had taught themselves to live decently, they thought that women continued to behave wildly. That was why they were supposed to need even stricter, continuous discipline from men. Kreon, a male character in one of Sophocles' plays puts it this way:

"There is no greater wrong than disobedience. This ruins cities. This tears down our homes, this breaks the battle-front in **panic-rout**. If men live decently it is because discipline saves their lives for them.... I won't be called weaker than womankind."

41

How Do We Know? Delphi

The landscape of Greece contains many ruins from ancient times. Along with Greek art and the surviving work of Greek writers, this archaeological evidence helps historians to form a clearer picture of the past. We know from Greek writings that Delphi was believed to be at the exact center of the world. In a steam-filled cave there, the Greeks set up the ancient world's most famous **oracle.** The most important person in this most sacred and important of places was a woman.

Words of the Pythia

You may be surprised that a woman, not a man, presided at Delphi. In this book, you have found out how small a part most women played in public life. Greek men believed that, since women were so "emotional," they could be very dangerous. So they tried to keep them hidden away and gave them few rights. Yet they also thought that by being so emotional, women were in closer touch with the supernatural. For that reason, women were thought to be better able to make contact with the gods and to listen to what they wanted **mortals** to do.

According to ancient Greek writers, on the seventh day of each month, a high priestess, called the Pythia, would sit on a sacred tripod. She would enter a trance. In her trance, she would listen to the questions of visitors from all over the ancient world and would then give answers that the ancient Greeks believed were inspired by the god Apollo.

This is an aerial view of the site of Delphi today. Two pieces of general advice from the god Apollo were carved in front of the temple: one was "Know yourself," and the other was "Nothing too much."

These answers were not always straightforward, and for that reason, they had to be interpreted by male priests. Nonetheless, in male-dominated ancient Greece, a woman held one of the most important religious jobs.

We do not rely on writing for our information on Delphi. Next to the oracle the ancient Greeks built a temple to Apollo, a theater, and a stadium for the Pythian Games. In 331 C.E., Aristotle and his nephew made a list of all the champions at the Pythian Games. These records were **inscribed** on four stone tablets that were found by **archaeologists** in modern times.

Here are two stories about responses by the Pythia at Delphi:

King Croesus wanted to know whether to go to war or to keep the peace. The Pythia said, "Go to war and destroy a great empire." Croesus went to war, but it was his own empire that was destroyed as a result.

Three Romans, Lucius Junius Brutus and his companions, asked what the future held for them. The Pythia said, "Young men, he among you who first shall kiss his mother will hold the highest power in Rome. Brutus bent down to kiss the ground, or Mother Earth. In 509 B.C.E., he became First Consul of Rome, the city's chief **magistrate.**

Today, tourists from many countries around the world visit the ruins of Delphi, following in the footsteps of countless ancient Greek people who came with their questions for the Pythia. In some ways, the ruins themselves are now like oracles, showing us secrets not of the future, but instead of the past.

This painting from around 440 B.C.E. shows the priestess Pythia sitting on the sacred tripod, in a trance. Perhaps the man pictured here is waiting for answers.

Timeline

All the following dates are B.C.E.:

c. 3000–c. 1450	Greece is controlled by Minoan kings from Crete.
c. 1600–c. 1100	Greek-speaking Mycenaeans rule separate kingdoms in mainland Greece.
c. 1100–c. 800	Greece goes through a period of wars and migration.
c. 800–c. 700	Homer's *Iliad* and *Odyssey* were probably written; Greece is made up of small city-states that are ruled by separate kings or noble families.
c. 750–c. 550	Greeks set up colonies in lands around the Mediterranean Sea.
c. 500	Some city-states become democracies; of these, Athens is the most powerful.
c. 490–479	The main period of **Persian** invasions of Greece occurs.
431–404	The **Peloponnesian** War, between Greek city-states, ends with Sparta eclipsing Athens as the most powerful state in mainland Greece.
378–371	Sparta is eclipsed by a new power, Thebes.
336–323	Greece is ruled by Alexander the Great of Macedon after his invasion and conquest.
146	Greece becomes part of the Roman Empire.

More Books to Read

Barron's Educational Editors. *Greek Life*. Hauppage, N.Y.: Barron's Educational Services, Inc., 1998.

Bartole, Mira, and Christine Ronan. *Ancient Greece*. Parsippany, N.J.: Pearson Learning, 1995.

Clare, John D., ed., *Ancient Greece*. New York: Harcourt Children's Books, 1994.

Day, Nancy. *Your Travel Guide to Ancient Greece*. Minneapolis: Lerner Publishing Group, 2000. An older reader can help you with this book.

Ganeri, Anita. *Ancient Greeks*. Danbury, Conn.: Franklin Watts, 1993.

Malam, John. *A Greek Town*. Danbury, Conn.: Franklin Watts, 1999.

Nardo, Don. *Life in Ancient Greece*. Farmington Hills, Mich.: The Gale Group, 1996. An older reader can help you with this book.

Pearson, Anne. *Ancient Greece*. New York: Dorling-Kindersley Publishers, Inc., 2000.

Rees, Rosemary. *The Ancient Greeks*. Chicago: Heinemann Library, 1997.

Glossary

archaeologist person who studies buildings and objects from the past to discover how people lived

assembly gathering of Athenian citizens who governed the city

barbarian anyone who was not Greek

barracks building or buildings in which soldiers live apart from other people

betrothed engaged, promised in marriage to someone

citizen person with the right to take part in politics, in particular, by voting

civilization distinct way of life that is common to a particular group of people

colony settlement in one place by people from another place

deity god or goddess

dowry marriage gift from the bride's family, consisting of money, land, or goods

fillet narrow band for binding the hair

hearth floor of a fireplace and the area around it

heiress girl or women, usually a relative, who is given wealth or property from a person who has died

inscription writing carved into a surface, such as a monument or a coin

lamentation grief-stricken wailing

license freedom or permission to do something

loom machine for weaving yarn or thread into fabric

magistrate officer in charge of enforcement of the law

mortal living creature, such as a human, that can die. The opposite of this is immortal, meaning able to live forever.

mourners people who grieve for one who has died

myrtle plant with dark leaves, white scented flowers, and black berries

oracle place where people could consult their gods for advice or prophecies

panic-rout chaos caused by fear

papyrus material used as a writing surface, made up of reeds

patron protecting figure

Peloponnese southern region of mainland Greece. This region includes the city-state of Sparta.

Persian person who lived in the ancient Middle Eastern kingdom of Persia, which is now known as Iran

philosopher person interested in thoughts and theories, from the Greek words meaning lover of knowledge

polis (more than one are called *poleis*) Greek city-state

rational sensible, sane

reputable known to be respectable

rite special celebration, often at a religious festival

ritual special, often holy, way of doing something

rouge substance used to color lips and cheeks

sacrifice ritual slaughter and cooking of an animal in honor of a god

sacrilegious offensive to something sacred, against holy law

seductive appealing, tempting

segregated kept apart

shift woman's dress, often loose fitting

shroud cloth used for wrapping up a corpse

spouse one's husband or wife

status position in society

taboo forbidden thing

tragedy serious play about a serious subject

wet nurse woman employed to feed a baby with her own milk

yarn any kind of thread that has been spun

Index

3214